Architecture of Dust

"The poems in Chike Nzerue's *Architecture of Dust* attend to the senses in the ways only a physician-poet can: that is to say, they blur the boundaries between feeling and intellect, sensation and abstraction, and so forth. The result is a collection that resists the intelligence, as Wallace Stevens exhorts, 'almost successfully,' and in doing so, guides readers toward a space of underexplored experiential terrain. Moreover, though Nzerue is a Romantic at heart — nods to Keats abound — he never gives in to that mode's troubling flourishes or indulgences. Rather, these poems bring us to the edge of reality full of pain, but rather than beautify it, or look away, they invite us to probe the intricacies of strong feeling, revealing its centrality to human feeling and human being."

—John James

"The best of these poems sparkle with arresting images and recall Okigbo's incantatory power. Nzerue displays versatility as he fashions memory, myth, and history into poems that evoke innocence, nostalgia, and loss."

—Okey Ndibe, author of *Foreign Gods, Inc.*

"Chike Nzerue is a master smithy of pleasing sonic combinations. '. . . of a centurion in the salt wars of abstinence / that covered enough miles to make Pheidippides jealous,' he writes. I find myself basking in the afterglow of assonant combinations. This book is a pleasure!"

—Kyle McCord, author of *Reunion of the Good Weather Suicide Cult*

"If there were ever a collection that captured so elegiacally one's interactions with and responses to the intricacies of love, belonging, death, and acceptance, Chike Nzerue's *Architecture of Dust* is just that book. Largely written from a physician's perspective, Nzerue's poems examine the fragility of our bodies, looking at the death of a sibling, the remorse that follows a misdiagnosis, the often predictable and debilitating effects of middle age, and the harsh realities of cancer. But Nzerue's talent lies in his ability to move beyond the clinical lens, and whether traversing the speaker's home continent of Africa, the U.S. Midwest, Las Vegas, or the mazes of the human heart, *Architecture of Dust* always focuses on what one can do to never let regret linger longer than it needs to. These poems are medicine for a wounded world. Here is our chance to heal."

—Esteban Rodríguez, author of *The Valley* and *Before the Earth Devours Us*

"If the physical body—its processes, its pain, its generational wisdom—has a language of its own, nephrologist-poet Chike Nzerue is its translator. In 'Stethoscope,' the ubiquitous tool becomes a metaphor for listening to the soul of both patient and physician—'When I lend you my ears, / you harvest rhapsodies / of wholeness / or glean blue songs / for the broken parts'—while in 'Henrietta Lacks,' the immortal Hela cell takes the place of Keats's Grecian urn as an occasion for a meditation on art, death, and truth (indeed, Keats' brief career as a surgeon's assistant is not lost on Nzerue). In addition to his medical references, Nzerue's artistic touchstones bridge past and present: here Tupac, Rihanna, and Nipsey Hussle take their places in the poetic pantheon alongside Keats, Dickinson, and Williams. *Architecture of Dust* is also a paean to Nzerue's native Nigeria, as well as a lament for the years spent away from it: this collection embodies the 'dueling seas' of geography and culture that meet to create a storm in the heart."

—Rachel Abramowitz

Architecture of Dust

Chike Nzerue

Leapfolio

Leapfolio
A joint-venture partner of Tupelo Press
North Adams, Massachusetts

Architecture of Dust

LCCN: 2022917364

Library of Congress Cataloging-in-Publication data is available upon request.

ISBN: 978-1-946507-09-9

Cover and text designed by Allison O'Keefe

Ribcage Torso Illustration ©GJD from Pixabay via Canva.com
Line Detail Flowers ©sketchify via Canva.com
Desert image courtesy of Kai Stachowiak

First edition: April 2023

Leapfolio, a joint-venture partner of Tupelo Press
P.O. Box 1767, North Adams, Massachusetts 01247
(413) 664–9611 / info@leapfolio.net / www.leapfolio.net
www.tupelopress.org

For Godfrey & Grace, my parents

Though still unravish'd bride of quietness,
Though foster-child of silence and slow time,
Sylvan historian, who canst thus express
A flowery tale more sweetly than our rhyme:
What leaf-fring'd legend haunts about thy shape
Of deities or mortals, or of both,
In Tempe or the dales of Arcady?

—John Keats, "Ode on a Grecian Urn"

Heavenly Father, We are Dust—
We apologize to thee
For thine own Duplicity—

—Emily Dickinson, "'Heavenly Father'"

CONTENTS

Part I
Tulips & Breath

What Is on the Line? 3
Ode to Breath 5
Lost Boy of Davidson County 6
Stethoscope 8
The Run 9
One Myth 10
A Prayer for My Brother 11
Hiss of Oxygen: Silent Hypoxia 12
Lip Reading Behind a Mask 13
Blues for a Face Mask 14
How to Break Tulips 15
Henrietta Lacks 17
Prostate Cancer: A Love Poem 18

Part II
Special Topics in Dust Archaeology

House of Dust 21
Mediterranean Dust 23
Dust Hill & Weeds 25
A Love Call to Dust 26
Dust of Little Africa 28
Dust Alphabets 30
Rhino Elegy 31

Part III
Singing American Rivers with Langston Hughes

Flint River Anthology 35
The Mountain in My Blood 37
Belle Meade: A Plantation between Two Rivers 38
Middle Age Is a Blue River 39
Elegy for Nipsey Hussle 42
How to Get Away with a Lynching 43
Tupac's Vegas Spot 45

Part IV
Prodigal Son Blues

Blues for a Prodigal 49
Grandma's Cashew Tree 50
Where Is That Accent from? 51
Hibiscus 52
Hanging of a Stateless Man 54
Africa is Not a Country 56
Mama's Boy Homecoming Ghazal 58
Blue Raindrop 60
Njaba River Trip 61
Trees in the Harmattan 63
Ode to Nigeria 66

Notes 71

ACKNOWLEDGMENTS

I am indebted to my poetry "posse"—Kathie, Marion, & Buffy, who saw my "ugly lines" and helped polish them into poems.

Part I

Tulips & Breath

What Is on the Line?

Like an Opelika line dance, words are asked
To jiggle off the page.

Wearing its heart on its sleeve, such heft
Swaggering a ponderous tread of trochee.

The dance moves magical, metrical,
Like madrigals, yet

Somber & bluesy as a down-
Tempo boogie woogie.

Each line made to bench-
Press pain and blues alike,

Open & close heart
Valves, and light shines

Through the mind's eyes,
Through those seas

Bearing the searing lash
& ecstatic gash of its rules.

Sing the dance & refrain
In sambas of alliteration,

Wield double-talk into
The blossom of couplets—

All it's got to lose
Hangs by this ruse:

Haul a dope world of plot
On a guitar string, bent as B.B's Lucille.

At the world's end, lines must fall
Well before verse & song.

Ode to Breath

Roil of pistons & bellows—

this orgy of empty and fill—

so much of it silent

inflation & deflation, seize
& release within a cage of ribs—

winged airflow, a blown kiss

(rustle of dry leaves

supple and softer than a hiss)

blued only by a

conspiracy of pollen & mites

drinking breath through straw

so despair rattles lung branches,

heart-shaped mouth agape—

Lost Boy of Davidson County

Before I could hold
or name you, you sailed away

to the waters of Nashville—
lost in the arms of two rivers—

one confederate, one union—
what did I know about how scarce

the father's shadow casts
before the son's light is out.

Famished & torn yet
strong I stayed for your mum,

pruned to a dark granite,
shoulder of a father bearing clouds

in his head, through morning walks
round old Hickory Lake's ripples

playing *Marco Polo*, our layaway game
of searching for hidden violets—

blue with dreaming.
Finding them, I find you pulsing

through that ultrasound—
they look at us and I see red wreaths

shaped like question marks,
Why you left and I stayed?

You arrived in blood, conceived
in East London,

a night without armor
and left in trickles of red—

breaking three hearts
that beat so singly—

in the art of drowning a sky
under slate, lowdown water.

Stethoscope

Black sidekick, Laenec's
bequest, coiled like a mamba,
a man in a white coat
lost in a field of poppies.

Apart, we're mired in bleak
straits, like Keats's lines—
together, ventriloquist
& dummy, powers imbued
like the staff of *Hermes*—

When I lend you my ears,
you harvest rhapsodies
of wholeness
or glean blue songs
for the broken parts.

The Run

The diagnosis—high blood fell—
like a gavel, ending the marathon trial
of a centurion in the salt wars of abstinence
that covered enough miles to make Pheidippides jealous.

Runs timed by watches & sweat,
to escape the shadow's loom—
The same wolf stole my mother's last son
in a moth-smoke of eclampsia.

I grieve for slices of pizza & soups
passed up—

Both grandpas died from heart failure.
Uncle Inno—an aneurysm.
While I ran, the genes held
the hourglass in place.

One Myth

Find pitchforks, fence in lakes,
mire the self in storm and split heart.
To topple a myth requires doubt
plus a stone that shakes and wracks
the marbled part, just as friendly foes
mock the racket it makes.
Perhaps the rules needed brakes—
exceptions that rent not apart—
To topple a myth takes an effort
that shakes sticks at freedom,
that highest art waylaid
in its own capital, which makes
sense, lest we find what it takes,
and lose that which tears us apart—
To topple our myth it takes
all the comedy of errors we make.

A Prayer for My Brother

That I was not there when you died
tightens me, like a knot.

Your generous lungs afire
singed to ground glass—
ruins, a Carthage of despair.

Our pact, Gibraltar strong, now broken,
haunts like an abscessed tooth,
our double solitude, its token.

I want to pour the red aged
wine over the broken
years we shared,

relive the teenage foibles
that lit our souls across
so many cobblestone miles—

pulsing like the core
of a new-made star, faraway
battened by black heaven's purr.

No art to throat
the choky heartbreak—
Sorrow's rucksack & coat.

I trail your ghost, claim
the sweetest verve of our past,
and rue what's lost.

Hiss of Oxygen: Silent Hypoxia

We sent him home
to recover in isolation,
no fever, just a crack-bark cough,

unseen, a lung filled with spikes,
as though primed for a siege—
Lung rattles hushed in sleep,

no risks but life—
oxygen & carbon dioxide
playing Russian roulette.

I, the healer, fooled
by his swan-like calm,
called it wrong—

Their love still strong,
if flowers pale & stale—
His wife's tears, my bitter pill.

Lip Reading Behind a Mask

It's a blue art
to garden words,
catch their slippery drifts,
or read their hieroglyphs
behind a blue mask—
to unearth the diamond
in their coal-dark gaol.
They that in times past
loved hard & softly kissed,
now puckered in dread compact—
read marbled, numb lips, lost cigar,
flashlights, salt of cryptic tears—
read their pantomimed prayers.

Blues for a Face Mask

In ancient Igbo culture,
wooden masks with plastic smiles
connect living & dead, blue
bow & salute to ancestors.

This N-95 is my shield
of faith & talisman
against loom of sky-sized
dread & aim of invisible arrows.

My breath purrs through
it, bending light
beneath the glass castle
that hides my marbled lips—

uses me like a pimp
as I step deep
into April's cruelty,
a silent, viral spring.

How to Break Tulips

> Here are platoons of gold-frocked cavalry,
> With scarlet sabres tossing in the eye
> Of purple batteries, every gun in place.
>
> —Amy Lowell, "A Tulip Garden"

Give them whorls like Chinese alphabets.
Give them namby-pamby, for heart.

Load their stamens
with spiked contagions

in colors that boom
like a dozen cannon

& slam into hospitals.
Move triage to parking lots.

Give them the high-yellow
of last-ditch Dutch blooms before

the splendor of a flameout
in a blaze of glory—

as attacks go viral
& grief sticks like glue;

To blow a wrack through
nursing homes and ricochet

like stray bullets minting
orphans and widows—

suffer the urn-shaped tulips
to shatter their sulfurous bulbs—

as blanched petals crane
their necks to see corpses

piled mile high
in refrigerated trucks

in Elmhurst, incandescent
funeral pyres in India.

Overrun the favelas in Rio
to wreak havoc with carnival season—

empty the double-decker buses
in London's West End

where blanched petals hide
their bruises with pink mascara.

Constrain the afflicted
behind glass & aliquots of time.

This valediction of silence
that forbids mourning.

Henrietta Lacks

How fast the cancer cored your cervix
like an apple & stumped your docs—

You knew you were dying,
and like Persephone,

the earth cleaved to seize you,
while you gathered flowers,

your fears behind your brown eyes,
lips stiff as marble.

You played Calypso, promising
immortality to the Odyssean tumor

for abiding with you
as you plotted to shatter

a red ceiling to end the strife
and leap to the moon, leaving

us your immortal Hela cells,
and telomeres that jinxed the world.

Prostate Cancer: A Love Poem

Poseidon led us past that Red Sea
haunted by twists & turns,
jaw-breaking words flailing against waves—
hard spot on rectal exam,

PSA and back pain,
biopsy & second opinion—
all falling like monsoon rain
in your crabby bed of thorns.

Our victory seemed Pyrrhic
from the wounding passions—
of the four-armed *da Vinci* robot
that spared nerves & shot mine.

I escaped being neutered, but
learned to wear Depends
and bear more tubes
than a Roman aqueduct.

An unspooling Odyssean scrapbook
trailing a tale of gifts—
both epic & mundane
that lets our lover prosper

even in alteration and skirt
of doom, without so much
as a wreath of words—

Part II

Special Topics in Dust Archaeology

House of Dust

The dust-glimmered porch hosts
a yellow jacket's nest—

its front door kick-scarred
& the hinges shriek

their rust-cry salute at
your gentle shove

of steps to the kitchen—
a catacomb of pizza boxes

furled like scrolls
reeking of stale beer—

as you stop for a drink on
the dining table wreathed in dust

where our names are written
in kid-scratch, wiggly cursive.

Ignore the echo of your steps
through empty kids' rooms

to the living room strewn
with yoga mats & our

unfinished chess game
on the yellowed laptop—

all that thinking deep-sixed
like a furred, fractured flute.

Ignore the dank bedroom
that bent light to black holes

& close your eyes, on your
way out, lest you behold

the front lawn flying
a bunting of weed flags.

Mediterranean Dust

Spurred on by forlorn dreams
curated by smugglers for wads
of cash & smokescreen of prayers,

they crashed against waves,
& a sea that failed to part
into their doleful abyss.

Youth dropped like stones—
rent asunder from
ripped rickety skiffs in groans,

to find life at the sea floor
where no one worries about
the broken china of dreams.

But lie together
each to his own, next
to statues of Greek & Roman gods.

Refugees of Midas
Pyrrhic reprieve won
at last from poverty's gaol—

Africa, bleeds suns
in a red steady gush
of arterial blood,

while grandparents read
a new bedtime story
to kids who never cry

in quaint villages—
about how paper boats
are weighed down by grief rain,

but arise to lullabies
& ask if those buried at sea
never die, like the baobab tree.

Dust Hill & Weeds

—After Natasha Trethewey

Here, beside this toppled graveside
   dust sculptors work their alchemy
tilling sand & tending dust
   in that rondo of breath & soil—

a Fall day, half undressed in gray.
   Ten years since that homecoming
phased in like the moon, to a quaint abode
   where termites rule in janitorial frenzy

sieving, grinding & flipping grime
   until an anthill rose,
like a skyscraper from their subterranean
   city of hope, my reminder

of that winged gift of yours—around me
   nothing but speargrass & nutgrass.
My generous Papa giving back to earth,
   daring me to weed or flatten the hill,

unsure which way to please the man
   who taught me to love & raise pigeons,
but flew away like a dove before I could love back—
   & I fell, like a meteor into a cold dark hole.

I carry the stone you passed through this canvas
   between sky, dust, & leaves of grass
& what they kept to themselves, this anthill,
   the weight of earth on my heart.

A Love Call to Dust

When he was little, his pop
said, *Men, leave home to fend*

for the tribe, but behind
his back, great aunt Nnedi

shook her head, wistfully,
home, she sighed, heart cocooned,

leaving blossomed to loss—
Years later, when her son died

fighting in Burma,
Nnedi took to circling

her hut seven times, each morning.
The frightened roosters counted.

She trotted as if hoping
by the end of her walk,

her son would have swum
two oceans back to her

raffia-thatched hut.
No one knew about PTSD

back then, & that a black woman
whose son died fighting

the second World War for an Empire
that denied him would get it.

No matter, she yelled his name
until breathless & the wounded

Njaba hills echoed doleful peals
back to her, a call & response—

picking at the scab of her wound.
The owls hiding in the palm trees

mocking her calls, but not even they
could break her routine—Her cries,

Penelope's blues to a kid who found flight
but soared too close to the sun.

Dust of Little Africa

To the living we owe respect,
But to the dead we owe only the truth.

—Voltaire

Buried in sleep, I borrowed a handful
of ash between Greenwood's railroad

tracks to Africa & threw it
into the Nile, Congo, & Niger rivers—

& took their silt to rebuild North Tulsa
of 1921 brick by brick.

Skating on the heels of history
my eyes chafed & burned

from plumes of smoke
rising from Black Wall Street—

as I fluttered the avenues of Greenwood
like a hummingbird, before the fire & let

    North Tulsa speak of itself
in third person—

roaming the wide highways
of their nouveau riche dreams,

gallantry deferred & interred in dust
for a hundred years,

saluting the centenarians
who lived with ghosts

until they cleared their throats
of time's guilt-glittered phlegm.

Somewhere in their hearts
are rooms they still can't enter—

the ringing of those nights starred
with turpentine bombs

ringing like manic bells
In Transylvania—

shots fired by a militia
into a church—

the shatter of stained glass
and a new hymn to terror,

the yawn of mass graves
grieving absent headstones,

a homeland elegy
for Greenwood's lost Atlantis.

Dust Alphabets

Faithful & fateful janitor to
tinder or tender nature's wound,

who can doubt its ubiquity—
seen, invisible.

While we build citadels of glass
& chase utopia,

it claws back inch-by-inch
raising a mound, in grave, siren song—

Who can decipher alphabets of dust?
People ask Google;

Its syntax predates Gilgamesh
& shrugs at the Ferris wheel of centuries.

It knows what it knows—
that which we don't —

More faithful than the sun
sleeps deeper than death

decked in its golden garb
of rust & senescence—

Rhino Elegy

—After a documentary on poaching

In Krueger National Park, a black
rhino bull lay beheaded,

colossal behemoth on the plain,
a biological formation

or dwarf hill on
no ranger's map;

a point & kill
open wound—

with sawed off horns
& a crimson trail

mirroring the bull's death march—
painting forest brush as eyelids.

A collage in a verdant grove
sketching horrors of its hours

at the poacher's hands—
reduced now to a feast for hyenas

& vultures and startled
hordes of flies.

A crash deprived of its
bull—or patriarch—licked by greed

& a bull's throat closed
with doleful sighs & thrash.

Who shall miss its rude voice,
ink-black, sad-eyed, & bark-like hide?

A regal beast felled for
its horns.

Part III

SINGING AMERICAN RIVERS WITH LANGSTON HUGHES

I've known rivers:
I've known rivers ancient as the world and older than the flow of human blood in human veins . . .

—Langston Hughes, "The Negro Speaks of Rivers"

Flint River Anthology

They had no way to know
about the pestilence

of running water from
a slime-scummed river

that leached lead from pipes
to poison their kids.

They were strong & tough
like their brick homes

that became stone boats,
a necklace of thorns—

There are clouds in their
mother's eyes that hang

like tropical depressions
on the verge, unleashing

brown kids in bundles
like blue petals dipped

in dark flint river lost
in childhood's warm seas;

born at GM's birthplace, heir
to the great American future,

stuff of dreams or so
their mothers thought—

what did they know
of poverty's dirty secret?

Catch them young
scald their skies vermillion

& roll them up like Kleenex
while Flint's fountains weep.

The Mountain in My Blood

It flows between myself & me,
still, this wide river of pain
that runs deep
with witchery enough
to wreck the boats and bridges
of my body—
Its foothills are my joints
& their leaks and creaks
that bleed my spleen.

Mossed by valleys shadowed
in doubt, next to a jungle,
this lichened peak
towers above me—
a cup, unbargained for,
holding my life, its floods
in the hands of gods

whose boredom ferries
a silent tumult of flotsam
& sorrow over the summit
until donkeys & mules
return them to me.

Belle Meade: A Plantation between Two Rivers

So much had changed, except little—
There were pictures to prove it.
The mansion's earth tones
head to toe chilled the soul's warmth.

A story line now tweaked—
Heavy on thoroughbred
horses, & lineage to Kentucky
Derby winners, a version of *states' rights.*

Slick bleach-washing of
crimsoned sods, yet I hear
the tread of ghosts haunting hearts
like Banquo's, creaking past cabins.

Blues ring ears bloody & parch
the mouth Sahara-dry as cloudy eyes
drown tears for a fallow field of the fallen
who once trod rows of white gold,

in chained sorrow. I'm deaf
to hoofbeats, float among them
in a long gray-light chain of shadows
& lashed backs—horrors of fields

and antebellum homes &
sapphire terrors buried inside
the thoroughbreds' tale—
greatest feat of Dixie alchemy.

Middle Age Is a Blue River

—After James Parker

It's not like the flight
of chirpy hummingbirds
from skeletal winter trees—

nor the barely
perceptible slip of rug
from beneath your feet.

It's more a river on the go
with no flock of nymphs
for the ride, all about flow.

You have to stay dry
to tour Gethsemane—
Garden of chaos, yet seize the day.

You marvel at the plumbing feat
of peeing, and wonder
how you ever took it for granted.

You confront the stranger
in the bathroom mirror
& dart your wicked wink.

No droop of cheeks
or hanging jowls & turkey neck
can steal your joy, though they try.

You have finally arrived
at the station to stand your ground—
little room for the soul's wolf.

If you were a city, you'd be
like Pittsburgh—tourists ignore
your mists & rivers—fine.

If you were a nation,
you'd be like Monaco or Cape Verde,
cool, clean streets—gem of a sod.

You know regret, that vintage
instrument that braids nostalgia
& double take into pressed flowers

as your frenemy.
You look staid, but inside
you ride the horns of a new puberty

where hormones humor you
by heading south like migrant
monarch butterflies.

You practice forgiveness
like yoga, especially
for the stranger in the mirror.

Pain, your body double
& buddy, lurks closer
than a shadow.

Death smiles at you,
woos you with pump fakes,
but you know you're a lame duck—
he's a deadbeat, but still your daddy!

Elegy for Nipsey Hussle

Our hearts sank in our throats
watching you march through
bloody streets armed only
with smiles & roses.

You wore devotion home,
that garland of danger with aplomb
& zeal until it seemed you'd devour time
like Compton's Tupac.

When you fell living
your heart's first love,
the hood, your muse
sang to you in her streets.

In songs of fervor that flamed
you returned to the city
that nursed you in life
& death, unlike Dante.

Rest well, lost sun—
Love was your madness
shared by the city's angels,
coiled in your rap tunes.

How to Get Away with a Lynching

—For Ed Johnson

Make the rope circular, like
the case to hang him.
Dredge up the rape accusation
that bloodies him into a cell—

It's for his protection.
Ignore his pleas of innocence:
The gallows never knew
a guilty soul!

Disdain the Supreme Court's
stay of execution—break into his cell
to bring justice closer & round up
the mob to watch—

Measure the right weight of rope
to lighten the burden
if she's unsure about who did
it; it's OK—she's traumatized—

Find the sturdy tree
with a stalwart branch
that keeps him bolt upright
until the breath cuts off.

Excite the mob to fever pitch
with dog whistles—
like pardon negro shit
& avenge rape—

Spook him with
choo-choo train whistles
carried by the wind
to the Tennessee River—

Make a fiesta of it—
with ice and frozen drinks
to beat the southern heat
& comfort spectators—

Get to the Walnut Street Bridge
and hang him there
so the Tennessee River
sings his blues, forever
flowing gently, clear as conscience—

Let the court eat
its heart out—
dress justice in proper clean
garb of white cotton.

Tupac's Vegas Spot

The silence of exit
boomed its own cannons
having been deathless

for your lifetime—
Why did it have to be
in Vegas, I ask

but you had a star to claim
& a lonely rat pack
to grant company.

It was a Hobson's choice—
Live the generosity your
Panther mama taught you well.

I had to visit that spot
between Flamingo & Koval
twenty-five years on to believe it—

in search of poetic
justice in your mamba eyes—
Sorry it took that long.

Like many, I believed
you lived still, like
Elvis, beating death's rap—

No chance to become
a supernova on return
to the ancestral river,

We commit thee
back to cosmic dust
from whence ye came.

Now it's monsoon here
and the heavens weep
the season's treason

for the gallant mariner
who sailed America's
Red Sea of slaughter.

Your back harnessed
before birth—
and all the while, in life.

Like Keats, your Orphic twin,
you left at twenty-five to confound
us with your odes,

your golden voice
still ringing in our hearts—
clarion as church bells.

Part IV

Prodigal Son Blues

Dedicated to Christopher Okigbo (1932–1967),
who first "shined" my teenage eyes with poetry's beauty.

Blues for a Prodigal

I shall be back–
Past tugs of sulfurous trails
& overgrown narrow paths–
And when I do,
I'll embrace the Njaba River
to wash away the dust
of my vagrant days
& let the African violets speak
before my cataracts
get their paintings in–
I shall kiss the bird-eyed wind
on both cheeks
& taste the salt of my tears.

Grandma's Cashew Tree

The droop of ripe fruits,
alluring as debutantes
looming high on that tree.

Fruits whose barrel symmetry
mocked the pride of pears,
their brilliant yellow tunic
like Icarus, daring the sun.

Teetering between thatch roofs
& hubbubs of birds, tolling time's knell,
her face lit with a wry smile
as she snared some to share,

until our faces streaked
with tears of joy, as
she taught us to plant
the question-mark seeds,

away from the mother tree—
Like the coming dispersion
of our family, like oil bean pods
with crack barks and hushed cries.

A tree in her meadow
And its accomplice, time—
wringing & shrinking her kids
with frugal seeds in green tuxedos.

Where Is That Accent from?

It hits you, fast,
loose & tremulous
like coconut milk waves
storming up a teacup—

a treason searching
for its felony,
fake British, bemoaning
a belonging pawned.

It hides indigo secrets
long as a rap sheet—
arguments about home
that I didn't start—

the stuttered blues
of Kunta Kinte's
distant cousin & doleful
sighs of betrayal from ancestors—

my gutsy barbarian, purple
tongue shuffling behind
ivory gates—a wound I recover
from slowly, like an alcoholic,

a sorrowful flutter & lilt
for the Igbo tongue
not passed to my American
kids—my stone.

Hibiscus

—For Chimamanda Adichie

A poet could not but be gay.

—William Wordsworth

Of flowers, most picaresque
& flirtatious
even when blue,
purple, heart-red,
sexual red, Rihanna lip-stick red—

Others rouged pink
but cast violet eyes,
flaunt fiery mango high-yellow
mascara with amber blooms

wide enough for van Gogh's
sleek links, latches & clasps,
or snow-white, delicate
as best silk from Xian.

A defiant resistance token
of anthocyanins & flavonoids
whose saffron blooms deck
Nigeria, North or South—

Enchanting meadows & footpaths
painting spring to green—
with beauty that darts
& seduces, like a forked tongue.

Some overdressed, like
strippers at a church bazaar,
violet fire goblets roll loose heads
with the wind's nudge,

allowing the nappy-headed
Voodoo blooms to stand
their apocalyptic high ground—
blazing on metal vines, as birds cry.

Each blossom, a raised champagne
flute, the fallen petals gay
as choristers who return
like saxifrage to break stones—

Their triumphant stamens
don their best hats
at Easter & the best *gelle*
at *Ashoebi* parties.

Your lithe frames
& blithe purple petals
that plied rivers with
crimson blooms.

In my childhood, eyes defy
cobwebs of meaning now—
A still-life wreath for our
fallen in that Biafran war.

Hanging of a Stateless Man

—For Tochi Iwuchukwu (1985–2007)

For nothing more than the chance
to dream in color
you stained your teeth
with dirty palm oil
to leave a mark—
seizing it, your way
even to the dishonor
of ancestors.

Avarice blurred
your vision
into the mousetrap
of cocaine, reckless in
your need for Midas's touch
your deal of damnation
was sealed like Faust's—
fault not in your stars,
but your chickens now
home to roost
in that foreign land
where it's illegal to chew gum.

Your anonymity overwhelmed
so much, they named you
a stateless African—
as if a country like Fernando Po,
Abyssinia, or Biafra.
Your swashbuckling strides
ebbed in woe at the gallows.

At dawn, that day
you sailed reality's quaint stream
bereft of oars—I, your kinsman,
bleary eyed kept vigil with the rain-
Brailled windows weeping for you.

Avarice was your blessed curse—
paid in wasted breath & blood.

Africa Is Not a Country

Africa is
a place
long
stiffed

of its
children, gems,
& coltan to
call others—

haunted by
the despair
of Western
discovery's wreck.

Africa is
not a verb
to make
bees angry

nor an
adjective
for jackass
tuxedoed penguins.

Africa has
long rivers
wailing over dams
& smoke thunders—

it is
not an
iconic eden
or tabula rasa.

It hosted
the first
genocide
for a billion euros—

before
the Armenian
the Jewish
the Rwandan

it mined
the uranium
for the
Manhattan Project—

it dreams
it sings
it gave
a heart first—

and shaped like
a heart,
it's a
state of

heart—
my
one & only
Ithaca!

Mama's Boy Homecoming Ghazal

Sleepwalked by dreams & wrack
of afterimages that come home—

botched ambush of Time, the god
on a prodigal trailing shadows home.

I confront a strangeness in grandpa's
Obi homestead & wonder if it's home.

I see a day undressed by a peacocked sun
flower lip, pollen burn & sweat of home.

A purple-garlanded Agama lizard at blissed-
out Love play nods: it feels at home.

The winding trails of old, now swallowed
by an asphalt river skirting home.

My father fled this abode, after his Troy—
that Biafra war, so mama built this home.

Riding my heart's anvil of wanderlust
that juggled losses close to home—

Regret's the cud I chew for bartering talking drums
for a golden fleece, inquisition far from home.

When her boys return as fathers of men
& stiff pours of tone & entropy, is it home?

In April's rising, kind light, Chike sees her
smile petaled on blossoms at home—

When church bells peal as roosters
crow, I know I'm home!

Blue Rain Drop

A misty ache
raked away by the globe
on my lashes, round

like Giotto's O—a planet
hanging by a hair's breadth.
Its brittle knobs eye me with sorrow,

no swallows summer through
its hollow silver lining shrouding
pain, the way clouds hide wild rain.

If I blink, it'll kiss the earth,
a prismatic estuary is buried deep
in its heart, a tsunami rages

in its center—to wallow
in its Sea of Tranquility
is to drown—

Njaba River Trip

—After Gabriel Okara

You drew three hearts,
like an octopus
cutting through stones
of sullen hills
with granite shoulders
to find your trail
where roses bow.

Before that bridge arched
its back over you,
after a white man
unleashed the power of TNT
to topple insolent rocks—
hiding oracles of orphaned gods.

You, who washed away tears
through the Biafra years—
healing & soothing
with your slakes of thirsty chokes
salving sorrow's dirty linen
into Oguta's finger lake.

I carry the warmth
of your cold embrace
like Aladdin's carpet—
until I return to your valley
where nascent buds blossom
on banks, like purple-frocked maidens.

You surge through me, my blood
maps your trip to the sea
that buried ancestors in water
& foreign lands—
but left large black holes
in our family trees.

Trees in the Harmattan

—After John Ashbery

How silent the groves speak
now, trees shined in ash
boughed in decks of silver

breaking up sunlight's
radiance into slick
angels rustling down

with wings entangled
by leaves to bless
flower & fruit

with vistas ablaze
in crystal, laced
in blooms of gray.

Neem trees & brush
desiccated to tinder,
wear foggy hair

& sing bonfire anthems
to save the forests,
reminding us of our parents.

A season of winds
that streak & tread, casting stones—
shaking loose the musk

from skeletal trees
with bowed limbs held up
like lyres, mourning loss.

Iroko oaks bereft of crowns
like deposed kings, stand stock-still
wearing skirts of fallen leaves,

but find themselves moving
patch by patch in sync
With with the Sahara's soft pipes

like Birnam Wood
to Dunsinane, as lilacs
slump over stilled grasses.

Gutters & ponds are licked
dry by ravenous sweep
of the rapacious wind.

Groves ghettoed by trees
embroidering themselves all over
with olive-brown leaves—

rattle owls, those envoys
of woe & wrangle breaking
open what the season conceals.

Drought falls like despair
that only leaves and love brake
& raked leaves

drop in streams
floating to their own
Byzantium of delirium.

Vultures figure-eight skies
over forest fires and trees
like lovers spooned in languor—

mull this tease
from sky gods:
enchanter & wrecker
of time's seal on nature's pomp.

Ode to Nigeria

Combed by dueling seas, warm & cold,
Atlantic & Saharan,

yet, the exile island of my heart—
whose unnamed mountains I climb,

collecting wildflowers & stuffing
pockets with stones.

I want to be mired in your
kinky mangrove swamps

like a lover's tresses
before roaming

your thick forests, my soul
high as Iroko oaks

soaring fearlessly free
through your lush

exuberant savanna
like green, brown-eyed eagles

& count stars in sheep clouds
on your dark nights—

before the foggy rains
that make lagoons of creeks

& hide that woman
in the moon's face.

I want to giddy up
in the colorful horse

parade of Kano's Durbar
through Fagge's sunflower fires.

I want to ride your wistful
trade winds wagging

their tails & winking as
the Sahara flicks off heat

with fingers of that wind,
yet never asks the sun

for a break & just marches on
to a date with the sea.

I want to hop Atlantic beaches
like area boys & drink mango juice—

haggle hard for cowrie shells
& akara bean balls

like a marketplace gangster,
until I meet her

behind the baobab tree
to eat boiled peanuts

& drink palm wine—
beyond this sod of wreaths & wraths

looms the sorrow of division
streaming through the needle's

eye, spilling red ink—
I have lived your hate

& fled, yet return in love,
clutching pieces of your wreck.

I touch, like a beloved
at night, riding your curves—

from oil-soaked deltas
to blighted cocoa fields in the south

to the penguin-march of Sahara dunes
gleaming like a dirge up north.

NOTES

"Lost Boy of Davidson County"

Old Hickory: A lake in Nashville, Tennessee.

Marco Polo: A kid's game played around a swimming pool.

"Stethoscope"

Rene Laenec (1781–1826) invented the stethoscope circa 1816.

Staff of Hermes: The caduceus is the staff carried by Hermes, messenger of the gods in Greek mythology. It has two serpents entwined on it.

"Blues for a Face Mask"

Igbo masks are usually made of wood or fabric and are used in drama, social satire, funerals of royalty, etc.

"How to Break Tulips"

Inspired by an essay in the *New York Times* by JoAnna Klein (May 11, 2017) about viruses from China that attack tulip flowers and cause color-breaking effects. The tragic beauty of these tulips seemed to me a metaphor for the COVID-19 pandemic as it ravaged our planet.

"Henrietta Lacks"

A telomere is a compound structure at the end of a chromosome.

"Dust of Little Africa"

The Tulsa race riot occurred in 1921. Black Wall Street there was also called "Little Africa."

"Belle Meade"

Belle Meade is a plantation in Nashville located between the Harpeth and Cumberland rivers.

"Middle Age Is a Blue River"

This poem was inspired by James Parker's essay "An Ode to Middle Age," *Atlantic* (January/February 2020).

"How to Get Away with a Lynching"

On March 19, 1906, Ed Johnson, a young African American, was accused of the rape of a White woman, and murdered by a lynch mob, while legal proceedings were in progress to establish his guilt or innocence in Chattanooga, Tennessee. The mob defied the Supreme Court and lynched Johnson before his guilt or innocence could be established.

"Hibiscus"

A gelle is a headdress worn by women in Africa. An ashoebi is an after-wedding party in West Africa.

"Njaba River Trip"

The Njaba is a river in Southeast Nigeria. It has three headwaters. After Gabriel Okara's famous poem "The Call of the River Nun."

"Trees in the Harmattan"

Harmattan is the season of autumn in West Africa characterized by dry winds, dust storms, and cold weather.

"Ode to Nigeria"

Nigeria is sandwiched between the Atlantic Ocean and the Sahara Desert and is squeezed by both. Climate change is a big threat to Nigeria, with desert encroachment unleashing conflicts with killer herdsmen migrating from the arid north to the south. Many of Nigeria's mountains are unnamed and unsettled.

Durbar is an annual parade of horsemen riding through the streets of Kano to salute the emir-king. Fagge is a suburb of Kano, where I was born, where street hawkers sell flowers. The baobab is a popular tree in Nigeria that lives for hundreds of years. Palm wine is a popular drink in Southern Nigeria.

ABOUT THE AUTHOR

Chike Nzerue's poetry and essays have appeared in the Henderson, Nevada, *Writer's Bloc 10* anthology, *CHEST* medical journal, *American Journal of Kidney Diseases*, and *Voices of the Grieving Heart*, an anthology of poems about hope, healing, and loss from the COVID pandemic, among others. He is a graduate of Oxford University, and a former professor and clinical dean at Meharry Medical College, Nashville, Tennessee. He was born in Kano, Nigeria, and is a practicing nephrologist in Las Vegas, Nevada.

www.ingramcontent.com/pod-product-compliance
Lightning Source LLC
Chambersburg PA
CBHW020340170426
43200CB00006B/438